Free Verse Editions

Edited by Jon Thompson

PILGRIMLY

SIOBHÁN SCARRY

Parlor Press
Anderson, South Carolina
www.parlorpress.com

Parlor Press LLC, Anderson, South Carolina, 29621

Printed in the United States of America
S A N: 2 5 4 - 8 8 7 9

Library of Congress Cataloging-in-Publication Data

Scarry, Siobhán, 1972-
  [Poems. Selections]
  Pilgrimly / Siobhán Scarry.
     pages cm -- (Free Verse Editions)
  ISBN 978-1-60235-481-4 (pbk. : acid-free paper) -- ISBN 978-1-
60235-482-1 (adobe ebook)
  I. Title.
  PS3619.C277A6 2014
  813'.6--dc23
                              2013047584

Cover design by David Blakesley.
Front cover art: "Manifest Destiny!" (2011-2012) by Jenny
  Chapman and Mark A. Reigelman II. Image courtesy of the
  artists, Cesar Rubio Photography, and Southern Exposure, San
  Francisco.
Back cover art: "By the Bulrush" (2008), by Ben Grasso. Image
  courtesy of the J. Shonk Collection. Used by permission.

Printed on acid-free paper.

Parlor Press, LLC is an independent publisher of scholarly and
trade titles in print and multimedia formats. This book is available
in paperback and ebook formats from Parlor Press on the World
Wide Web at http://www.parlorpress.com or through online and
brick-and-mortar bookstores. For submission information or to
find out about Parlor Press publications, write to Parlor Press,
3015 Brackenberry Drive, Anderson, South Carolina, 29621, or
email editor@parlorpress.com.

Contents

PILGRIMLY

I

Hieratic

We turn Terpsichore under the refuse of wartime architecture, steel curve of the Quonset hut hiving over us. A historical embrace. You are all little quadrilles and makeshift foxtrots, my body making the shape of various nests. Earlier I pyramided plums in a bowl, fashioning forms that will serve no purpose. I am after the vestigial parts of the self. And the ones wholly invented by chance, location, available dressings for the exit wounds. A self is such temporal plastic and can be molded to serve a million gods. *Hamlet* in hundreds of theatres and prisons, and the skull speaks to every player. The way your grief hands move in coded succession, how the head is thrown back in laughter, other invisible genetic bombs that are ticking under our skin. To grow into something molded by other means. At dusk, small birds flit in the arch of galvanized sky, our tongues become sparring partners, and we are pulled into the animal attunements. After, I am salt-scrimmed, basalted, spooned into something like Smithson's jetty—all natural fashioning and fiddlehead curl, circling like an animal before sleep. Come, curate me into this rupture made of the made and forced and found.

Overture

Three rounded brass pedals and the thin bones of my mother's bare foot. Under the piano, she pushed down on the far right pedal. Chopin and Czerny opened like weather, and I went inside—where slim brick houses, where curtains were always drawn. When it rained in that part of New Jersey my mother's stockings would disintegrate on the line. I remember the heat, ice cream trickling its sugar juice down my wrists, when sleep would not come. A yellow swing and a root cellar with jars. Not everything had a language.

Residue

What is left of water: maps drawn on the arms after sunlight, white run of roads intersecting, to be tasted at night when the body is tired from rowing, a full day past lighthouses and seals that keep watch from the waves, the sea giving back a taste of my own skin. The tent is pitched under trees, arm muscles twitching in half-sleep— chalky feel of it in the hair, or rising up from the body during sex to pass from skin to skin, and the shoreline in Baja carved up to let it form on the land, landscape a winter white—residue—and we grow thirsty driving so far south in summer, our legs sticking to the seats and the brass bands playing from the radio of our rented car. These are the long stretches of white. In the evaporating ponds water leaves in stages and the land is divided accordingly, with shallow pools for the collecting. To turn into vapor, or to draw moisture out, leaving only the dry solid portion. There is a cathedral north of Bogotá that was once a mine. A long walk into the earth and what is left is the taste of the walls. We are not the only ones who hold the remainder in our mouths like gold. On the high passes at night, the curved horns of goats are lowering to the roads where we have passed. When we find them with our headlights, they tuck their tongues back into their watering mouths, give back the light with their eyes.

Attempts at Divination

Preparations for the unknown, shapes of buildings you've only dreamt, plants that will begin nameless. Even Lena's cards can't account for these forced turns, say nothing of camel, spoonbill, Urfa ibis. Forget these twisted black vines, mustard blooms between. In the old alchemies, *the whole earth is a booke . . . in which the pages are turned with our feet, which must be used pilgrimly.* If only we could read the marks our walking makes, words scraped onto the slow backs of turtles. How surely it moves beneath us, scriptura continua, our illegible lives.

Study in Light

to the outer reaches
the million bright million
refusals in the vein
tunnel in to these
old geometries, thick quartz
seams in the ladled earth
children waving branches
lit by company trust, new
plumbing, dry goods for every
worker put the lantern in, crouch
before the blast

Three Trees

For its red branches and because it grows here, on the banks of the Blackfoot and Swan. When I set it in the earth, I learned its name: red-osier dogwood. The book now tells me its Latin name, *Cornus stolonifera*. Meaning bearing stolons. The rooting of branch tips, which form new shoots when they touch the ground.

*

And what we called helicopters, the green twirling pods raining from maples, our palms outstretched to catch the red sun, the rake of bones almost visible through our lit skin. The true name is paired forking long-winged keys. And further: one-seeded, red or yellow when immature, turning brown in autumn.

*

Smooth stump of the gone tree, dark hole in the center, starburst splintering outward. Lay your hand flat against the thickness of air where it once grew: the coarse trunk, one arm reaching sideways with its inflorescence of pink-rimmed bunches seizing in bloom. It was so familiar you never asked its name: flowering dogwood, *Cornus florida*, cultivar "Amerika Touch-O-Pink." This and its truancy are what you now carry with.

As Longing Is to Lure

Thumbed through constellations until a bright assignation. Or was it always a self-induced fating, godheads and their freighted narratives, each belt and hairpin a moment of crux, as small and vital as the pivot point on Libra's double pan scale. There were stories you could choose as yours, and each would affix you to your own strap of sky. You were a woman or a word. Soon to marry, or refer.

Estuary

For its solitude, its slim salted rivers, the boatmen and their flat-bottomed boats. Here, only the wherries will fit. Blowsy grasses at the banks bend to drink, drown in the shallow water. Tips bleached in the surfeit. Vessels here need their skegs for navigation, to avoid drift and spin. And in the carved channels: oar pause, looms lift, sun glint. Then the blades back in.

*

Confirmation from the dictionary of shallow water: "The marshes are invariably deserted . . . . A seamless web of green undoubtedly pales beside roaring about the open ocean in an engine boat." No more silent gundalows for salt-hay, just one motorless boat aground on the mudflat, rudder dug in, keel over to the side. It will take only one spring tide. And more to see thanks to those who make seamarks —bleach bottle, beer can, stick jammed in.

*

The gift of your face on a flat skipping stone. How it took all night to render your own likeness. In summer we help the shoals switch their stones. Something from the other side making it across.

*

Navigation, visibility, sometimes poor. We fashion our family and it remains unsanctioned. Natal gatherings few and far. Years of goodbyes in gravel driveways do not form a pattern. Repetition does not always find its form. And in these days of distance, the dog remains our loyal, threading us together, pacing to knit the space, hoping for *pack*.

*

Gunnels up to breathing, the old soaked wood, the rib-bands expanded out like lungs. It will hold us through the unmarked channels, and what versions of ourselves will we see when we lean out over the water, our faces mirrored in the smooth aftermath of oarpull? On the creeksides, red-streaked grasses, microbial mats thickening on the banks, organics layering into patterns of the untrammeled (there are patterns in the untrammeled), our eyes now unstitched.

*

Full sea mark: "a line on a coast marking the tidal limit," or "an elevated object discernible at or from sea and serving to guide or warn mariners; a beacon; a landmark; hence a sign of danger." Let this remain approximate until an opening out into bright water, or a thinning into rills and spits. We remain in the crossing. Lean in to these shapes of the visible world, see what leaves itself for gathering, what pushes itself up to the wrack line.

By Water

The ocean spits up slick green pods and arranges them in awkward rows on the beach. The white of waves: the foam: the ceiling of gulls: the dim winter light that allows more brightness in. This was at the old farm north of the city and there were icicles at dawn that broke like thin sticks. Green towels, jar lids tightened with rubber-gloved hands, the candlesticks polished with worn cloths dipped in pink. At breakfast a woman said she was here to celebrate the one-year anniversary. She and the woman on the other side of the cloth partition had matched their breathing, timed their contractions together. The babies came out at the same time, one screaming with life and the other silent. *This*, she said at the farmhouse table. It was quiet now in the room and I was twisting my napkin. *This*.

*

By the river, clapboard covered in blackberry brambles, sharp smell of dormant vines, gray powder left in your hands. The guest journal, for some reason of place or lighting or perhaps the smooth quality of the paper, made visitors spill their lives onto the page. At least two people had lost their virginity in this bed, someone mapped out the breathless coordinates of sky, and a spider with a hard gold shell came through a knot in the wood and would not be moved. Other dreams, my clenched palms opening to these words: death is a clacking sound. And to explain I wrote, *like laying your ear on the factory floor all night, the sound of an endless stamping machine.*

*

The lake is filled with the bones of reindeer that missed the slight shift in horizon that would have told them *lake*. All here is white on white. The sound of thin ice breaking and the pewter-gray bodies sinking, branching antlers locking in slow grace, acoustics muted into hollow knockings. The fiddlehead ferns hold back the tips of their leaves with tight fists, and above, a raven inks his way across the sky, passing over again and again until the clear air takes the shape of his name.

Darkly

in the space
   between
longing

a lull,
  an absence
we mark

with chalkdust
    on the tips
of our fingers

grateful for silence,
      no sense
of slipping,

or the rocks that balance
   on each other
for centuries

no accounting
   for the permanence—

behind the iridescent answer
       of wings
there is more

humming,
        underneath
something rolling

and tumescent, a thunder
            binding matter
      and the jagged arcs

Still Life with Pomegranate

A single flushed fruit. The coaxing open of its many-chambered heart. To believe in the slow spill of bright arils into the palm. We were both in the landscape of waiting. Once we put up a bag of birdseed made especially for finches but they never came. It was affixed too high and close to the house. I would watch the full ripe bag of seed twist in the wind. There were promises and there were promises.

St. John's Parish, Bronx

We are far from that place now, the rattle of china in the rounded cabinet and two worn chairs with sunken shapes like your names. The pipes running up the walls of the apartment were hot to the touch, the whistle of heat coming through. The gathering and moments in between. I watched a team of crows work at a wasp nest, the gray papery cone unraveling slowly, thin paper sheets outstretched in the wind. The nest never came open. The gift of a slow careful build.

*

Over the telephone a clearing of throats and the rumble of above-ground trains and I could hear fear laying out the days, a nervous circling of hands for the way neighborhoods change, the way the tenement courtyard is always empty except for thick arms reaching out of windows and pulling in the wash. The glass eye on the door magnified our bodies waiting there with the side dish. And the storm milk makes when it hits the bottom of teacups.

*

Rosary beads are brought out from wooden boxes in the darkness and each bead touched. Your red hair let down and brushed a hundred strokes. I too remembered each tine of the dinner fork with the tip of my finger and running sticks along fences. The glass eye on the door clicks open when there is no one there and the saints on the wall sometimes fall, chalky, leaving scrapes on plaster from where they tried to hold on. When a bird flew into the apartment, a rush of hands pressed closed each open window and it was explained: the souls of the family were in danger of flying back out into the world. We were all in the same room once, the soda bread and tea, the two men in the family never speaking but the women kept the talk going and I never noticed. At night it was quiet except for the sound of that pearl-handled brush. And it was a fiery red until the end.

Jubilate: Burden, Kansas

For grain dust is fine and slips through the fingers.
For grain becomes bread that we break in your memory.
For grain is transported by ships and trains and long flat boats.
For grain is stored in buildings that rise up from flat land.
For grain elevators are strangely the poetry of the American sky.
For they are built in various shapes according to landscape and function.
For the buildings are pure in their geometry.
For the circle is unity.
For the triangle is the trinity.
For square and rectangle are pleasing in their shapes.
For the hexagon is the geometry of the bee.
For bees, in their building of honeycombs, gave rise to the schematics of
    interlocking grain bins.
For hexagonal bin design does not waste space—there is no need for the
    strangely shaped interstitial bins.
For the longest elevator in the world uses hexagonal bin design—Praise the
    grain elevator in Hutchinson, Kansas.
For elevators are made of many materials.
For we are woken to life by knowing decay.
For wood is decay.
For tile decays.
For steel bins do not insulate the grain.
For vermin get inside the bins and gorge themselves on the fine dust of harvest.
For life is decay.
For the abandoned silos are in decay.
For there is dust in our lungs.
For all creatures will come to dust.
For it is true—and I have seen it—that grain dust explodes.
For spontaneous combustion is proof of a Presence—Remember the thirty-
    three men who died at the Husted Mill in 1913.
For dust clings to elevators, even those converted to hotels and artists' lofts.
For firstly, the grain is moved upward in the elevator by small buckets on
    conveyor belts.
For secondly, the grain is moved to the distributing floor, where it is
    weighed and chalkboards mark the weight and grade and destination.

For thirdly, the grain is moved along conveyor belts and lowered into the
bins through small holes that the men try not to fall through.

For fourthly, the grain is stored for months or years or else it is moved
quickly through chutes onto boats or railcars waiting below.

For the storage and transport of grain is a wholesome enterprise.

For it is pleasing to feel the slip of grain between the fingers and hear it
crunch underneath boots on the cement workfloor—Be gracious to
the elevator in Burden, Kansas.

For each handful of grain comes from a field of growing things—Be
gracious to the cribbed wooden elevator in Attica, Kansas.

For fields from above are geometrically pleasing—Save the condemned
silos of Minnesota.

For there is Presence in the swish and movement of grain particles
colliding in the chutes.

For the storing of grain in large bins is the desire for tomorrow—Bless the
peeling letters of *C* and *T* and *A* on the silo in Lake City, South Dakota.

For the Dakotas are desolate and need their landmarks.

For those states have been spared with silos spaced evenly along the
railroad, every fifteen miles.

For people in Kansas are more needy—Bless the four-mile intervals.

For there is something to be said for the even spacing of certain
kinds of structures.

For it is important to love the spaces in between—Remember the
interstitial bins with shapes that accommodate.

For flat-bottomed bins are useless for unloading but have pleasing shapes.

For flat land must have shapes that rise up in praise. Bless Aldo Rossi.

For silos desire upward motion.

For the workfloor is the ground level—Praise the wooden elevator of
Chokio, Minnesota.

For the storage bins are the body of the building—Give us this day our
daily bread.

For the distributing floor has many windows but workers keep their eyes
on the floor to avoid falling through—Praise the buckling slats of the
elevator in Lucas, Kansas.

For the headhouse sits on top of the building—Bless the small dusty
windows of elevator headhouses.

For any structure so solid is a monument to the everlasting—A blessing
on Danville, Kansas, where the eighteen-bin silo dwarfs the church
(bless its steeple and the lonely slatted window).

For structures this large have SPIRIT inside them.

For SPIRIT is fullness.

For SPIRIT is round in its shape.

For round structures have no end and converge with the sky in an understanding of infinity.

For it is most common for grain bins to be round.

For common shapes are pleasing to the gods.

For storage is proof of thinking of tomorrow.

For allow me to consider a single spark in Wichita, Kansas.

For every spark does not ignite.

For desire cannot be predicted.

For sparks are in every careless cigarette lit on the workfloor.

For sparks fly from the steel rails of nearby train tracks.

For fire is the particular fear of grain elevator workers.

For fire CONSUMES.

For CONSUME is a word that feeds on itself, desires more than itself.

For the word keeps circling in the mouth when you are done saying it.

For a spark with the desire to CONSUME felled the DeBruce grain elevator four miles southwest of Wichita, Kansas.

For due to management negligence, on June 8th, 1998, a concentrator roller bearing seized from no lubrication and locked the roller into a static position as the conveyor belt continued to roll over it.

For this is called the "razor strop" effect—Imagine machinery at 260 degrees Celsius.

For these are the conditions that join fire with dust.

For seven men died that day for America's bread—Rest the souls of Jose Luis Duarte (41 years), Howard Goin (64 years), Lanny Owen (43 years), Victor Manuel Castaneda (26 years), Raymundo Diaz-Vela (23 years), Jose Prajedes Ortiz (24 years), and Noel Najera (25 years).

For even in its hell-bent desire, the spark could not reach all the bins.

For steel is strength.

For concrete is strength.

For the metal clasps on the lunch boxes are strength.

For the flat land is filled with structures that are still standing.

For when traveling in certain states, one elevator passes from view just as another appears on the horizon.

For elevators carry the eye upward to sky.

For elevators reach.

With a Line from Montale

Stubborn ditchflower bloom, trees threading the grooved culverts
upward—don't be done with this landscape: threshold of one part
land to three parts sky, and the mind at least can return to these
low-slung hills, velvet skin of summer turning to scorched grasses,
goldening—and the bright white limning of animal trails, scratched
like scars into these winter hills, these calibrations of, which you
carry carved in you as your sentence.

II

The Orpheus House

No, there is one small word printed in the center, paper unfolded three times, deep creases for markings on the empty page—read it over and over until there is no translation and it enters the body. Under floorboards we found things left and forgotten. Newspaper clippings, pens run out of ink, a small ceramic plate where stylized ideas of a boy and girl are not playing tennis. The boy is reaching out with flowers and the girl, kneesocks sagging, her racket tucked like a forgotten doll under her arm, stares out from the plate. There are no words on the maps anymore. Someone has pulled out the blue roads into long straight lines and the dots of cities have fallen to the bottom, given the string its weighted swing.

*

We sistered the joists under the kitchen so the floor wouldn't sag or slope, and it's true the inspector didn't have to use the level, the fear of three air bubbles listing in the liquid, pulling past center. Architecture has been practiced and perfected in your dreams, the building of something solid for the mutable world. We will have to adjust to familiar landmarks laughing from off-center. What remains fixed are the windows, the doors, the solid feel of the staircase on the way up.

Nine Threads

Follow the map of black tarmac cracks, rifts like riverbed, running for miles. The lift upward even brings it: moment of ballast stitched together with thick dread. In these momentary leavings, into some patch of mind is scratched a bright laboratory. Clearing through cloudstretch: aerial.

*

Landscape geometric, color-carved, flat land parsed into lived patterns. The farmer and his tapering fields, his neighbor in circular harvest, the tangents between. We will not visit the ones we glimpse from the sky, maps not collapsing to see for ourselves. Only this: clear relations from above. The transparent layer between.

*

Does it always take such time? There are days I drive so close to the coast. Birds of prey stock-still on their branches, scouring. Not all of us travel for the rush of ocean, but the brown furrows before. Hollow free twist of grasses and something quick that might require us. Am I the only one who feels this joining? The birds accomplish outside my field of vision, return to their aeries. I look up for what still waits on the wires, lean in to the curves. Triumph of the penultimate: somewhere before water, I always circle back.

*

Gather this from a different place. The sounds of sewing, subterranean now. Daddy longlegs in the egress window, testing the tops of the mason jars. A coveting of buttons. Fabrics wrapped tightly in their bolts lean against the wall, slip-shine. On the card table, thin brown paper is laid out like hope. Dotted lines: bright pulse for cutting. These were the first roads, sure and quiet, someone else's. Under the table the black pedal beat time, low hum, foot testing the ridged hypotenuse, cracked heel at the treadle, digging in for the stitch.

*

Red rusted pools, black underbloom, photograph of a weathered truck. No, it chronicles the broken: Silver Bow Creek where runoff from the mines pulls the land into *Superfund*. The photo taken from the belly of a plane over Anaconda, Montana. Aerial abstract.

*

We cut back in the spring, and so differently—your shears going to bone. When we lived in the city, you trimmed the lavender until it was nothing more than ropy gray trunk and tight little leaves. We waited a full year for the purple bloom. I am reluctant to do away with anything green, anything desiring itself. The lilacs are sending new shoots into the clean patch of yard and I will let them.

*

Raining, the backyard filling with mud, you reached out to feel my wings, damp and broken, gray feathers sticking together. I remember the aerial view of the dinner table, plates round as silos. You were always afraid of my hunger, and there were times I turned my head right in the middle of things. We could feel the pull of the backyard then, its suspension, its desire to release us with the furniture, sneakers missing their laces, the ice always breaking, making room for movement.

*

Trees still unsure circles, towns scratched into the earth at right angles, dark crease of the rail line running through. The land will give up certain secrets, but how to suture through the cardboard backings, how we are fixed—to place, under sky, mortgage, bulbs planted and wanting our tend. We save the rusted weights from old windows, but no longer know why. So much now unwoven. Everything we thought was passed down was lent.

*

I wanted a book that would bring me closer to the birds. Pages smelling of static and the careful tracings from bones, attempts at capturing songs with words. Most abundant: the Northern Mockingbird, nest made from twigs, mosses, string, and dry leaves. Found in shrub or vine tangle. Songs sung three times, sometimes more. We travel these roads, ours now, past white fallow deer, and the exhalations as we travel gather. Do the gatherings matter? Invisible waters from inside us collect on the windowpanes, and you trace our names. The land rushing by offers its burnished grass bloom, and moss catches on tree limbs like held breath. Months from now, winter will make the windows film, surfacing the originals. Will it be my name on the glass? Was it ever my name you traced there?

All Things Being Equal

True: this night without a moon, the rush of water far below, how everything seems to stretch beyond itself. You ask at the river, at ourselves mirrored there. We invent an errand and climb up the vacant hill, remnants of snow crunching under our feet, the small red lights of a radio tower guiding us up. There are hundreds of small branches keeping us from the more solid limbs of the tree. *I know there is more than just us*, you say again, though there are only two sets of breath-marks against the window, two sets of whorled fingerprints on all the objects in the house—book spines, ice cubes, volume control. It is almost visible tonight: where we came from: who we each were: and could be: before.

Interim

1.

At the border
no building
no planting of trees: craving
sightlines   we
idled in the car   our
passports open   still

2.

      lacework
makes of emptiness   designs
on the soul   do you feel
         pull

3.

Score the longing
           //
throat   its known
attachments   breath
a body
     waiting   [

4.

    if
fear becomes   you
delay   the lungs
fill   the calcareous
mind   in interim

5.

A circadian   weather
      of longing
reaches eastward   makes of time
a material

6.

Or wind up
watches to live in
lag time   vertical
lines I'd drag across
Nebraska   in my teeth
catch the slide   rule
of sun   in timed
brightness   threads
the needle: longitude

7.

Holding the space

8.

I have only this   orthographic
love   envoi
each day (an envelope)

9.

A train zippers   the night
tracks   gleam in parallel
lines we draw   the distinctions
a flinch   but you return
soft   //   edges

10.

In between   a life
apart   small ruptures
unravel   Penelope's
knot of lost time   inside
her virtue

11.

Empty
folders   rustling
the body's daily
accordion of   breath
unrecorded   silent
subject   of your regard

12.

Don't hold me   apart
I do this   shedding
too   a summer
cicada   burrows up
from   clings to
what stands   long after
chora chora]: we

7 Girls in Petticoats and Kneesocks (School Photo, circa 1920)

So the children are shadowed by parents. The photographer unschooled in the movements of the sun, dark stains of adult bodies in the foreground, loomy outlines at the tips of Mary Janes. O our whistling in the graveyard (tactic ditched). In the recurring dream we are playing with puppets, hands secreted inside. The animal mouths open and close, do the talking. He sips from a tall blonde beer until a sneeze takes his body shaking, expanding, blowing past roofline. Typical, the running chase. And the hands unsheathed, grown into monsters, the loud kind of grabbing. It's part of the old story. A father names his daughter Electra, hopes for the best.

Pantoum

Returning to the summerhouse
willful and patching the places
where light leaves, broken
storm doors, shafts of dustlight

willful and patching the places
the children left
storm doors, shafts of dustlight
bits from constant collecting

the children left
small things for the sill
bits from constant collecting
moss that holds the brightness

small things for the sill
the trails overgrown
moss that holds the brightness
inside the house

the trails overgrown
casting her shadow back
inside the house
a soundless shift of bodies

casting her shadow back
into a lithe unfamiliar form
a soundless shift of bodies
returning to the summerhouse

Pietà

The dog slips under the convent gate and the nuns want to keep him.
No matter the owner is pressing his finger to the buzzer all night. A
full-grown retriever, golden, and he puts his paw softly against the
sisters' knees when he wants to eat. How could they bear to turn
away this unexpected affection? The Sister sneaks the dog to her
room once everyone is sleeping, and lays out an old wool blanket on
the floor. His paws reach over the edge onto the linoleum and she
hears him all night, running in his dreams.

*

The smell of the bell tower draws her back, even when it isn't time.
Stone and old rope and something earthy like moss or dead vines,
and she is remembering the cellar in her mother's house. Rows of old
jars filled with preserves, the canned fruit floating like fish. His eyes
in the darkness when he led her there after dances, down the cement
steps, through the door with the old glass knob. In the coolness he
asked quietly where everything was contained, sealed and safely
waiting until winter. She made a deal with Saint Theresa whose
ecstasy surely came from letting go.

*

They are tracing the path of earlier pilgrims but miss a few sites
because they travel by train. She looks out as they shuttle through
fields of lavender, bruised purple blooms swaying in unison, away
from the tracks. She has seen pietàs in marble and alabaster, rough
stone and wood. In every shrine, stray dogs roam through pews in
search of food. When she enters the grotto in St. Baume, the air cool,
water dripping down stone, the sound—take, drink—becomes siren.

Walker Evans Meets His Subject (*Grave,* 1936)

Hundreds here, all above ground, the earth too hard and dry for digging. Each grave is an oval of packed soil, crude boards for markers and no names. You can tell the women apart by their dishes, which lie at the crest of each mound, on display. I unscrew the lens cap and walk among them, the milk-colored pitchers and blue bowls, a shimmering iridescent vase. The soil is pocked from an earlier rain as if two young girls had dug their small fingers into the thirsty Alabama dirt. Shadows crawl long over the soil, bringing up something of the darkness below. The light now is perfect. I choose you for the shallow white bowl, because it is leaning slightly and sunlight is hitting the thin rim. Is there bread still rising on the sideboard? The light is already changing, changed. You follow me into the next frame and the next and into every photograph I take: thin blonde hair pulled back at the neck, the white bowl resting on your hip, you are calling out from the porch to your girls, brushing the dirt from your one good dress.

Elegy

—after 9/11

The boats of his childhood still circle. Liberty Park to Battery Park and back. It was always more than thermometers could measure. On breaks in the tight maritime bathroom, he saved himself with ice-filled cups and secular texts, both of which he pressed into service with quiet reverence, as if in prayer.

*

So much needed mending. The faces of people up from tunnels, blinking in the new light. Bright silences and memory of metallic bloom, the waking of reptile brains.

*

It was late when they rode to the top of the towers. The children were lifted to the owlish faces of view masters. River of red lights, green. Those who pressed their faces to the dull silver saw the city and believed then in design, in the shapes surrounding each small life.

We Meant to Ask the Machinery

Before the edifice, uplift: wrist hinge unfolding, gentling its gift of gravel. High-hat pile drivers, muted by liquid thick. And the watermarks confirm: a cementing underneath, fish darting, displaced. The harbor extends. You number your sailors and birds as if numbers might comfort. The boat's name is Relief, though it's beached in the mucked shoal of bridge support. The photograph (interrupt—a boat named Blue Flasher passes, white-lit, salt-scrimmed gear mountaining the aft) we were meaning to speak of: diptych of a cantilevering. Such sturdy equipment on the pier, numbered train cars (as if), and how the gasolined necks of the pigeons (not pictured) shine.

Living Room

All tensile shine with an internal quiver. A weather that does not wear itself on the outside. Sibilate and search, sound the drum of the ear that scours the silence. The past has dragged its monstrous feet into every new room. Each surface revealed as teeming agar: circuitry of atomic life, germs in their palimpsestic rigor. How surely we twine our idiot secrets into a knotted thing that tugs the root of each heart clear of its chest bed. Fitting, the framed lithograph of the traced and labeled parts of an anonymous heart: left ventricle, atria, mitral valve. The oldest languages are spoken here, though we lack even the bluntest tools of translation, able only to cradle the infant babble in our own ears. If sunlight moves through this room, it is only the work of obligation.

Littoral

Still it calls me and the *what if* and the snow moving back beyond the garage. Did we always want this? The clippings sent to ourselves to grow in water and the shallow pools that uncurled the leaves, made something whole and then it was time to gather more. You were always in charge of the excursions. Tidepools, red swaying fingers from the sea that coiled from our touch. I trained the eye of the telescope to watch the sea grass whip in the wind, instead of the foam or birds or neighbors in their windbreakers. The knowing has come late this time and still it is not a clear path from the house. In each crunched footprint, a shallow pool of water is cupped, collecting small bits of winter sky. If I drag something heavy behind me the pools will gather in a steady stream, will carry a whole cloud through to the other side, and the silence waits   for me to go back   and find a key somehow   to hear while it waits   and takes me   and brings us inside it   to hear what   is.

After Blackdamp

Floating free across the fences that separate the empires of our backyards, each particle of dust alive and lit with summer. Feet skittering in shale slide, moccasins stuttering on the shallow creek water, and the children's children of the Pennsylvania miners caper in aboveground air, white flesh of their feet bloaty and wavering under the blurry microscope of free time. Permission to run full tilt toward the last blink of firefly, to the light-charmed trees in the far fields. These new bodies are free from blackdamp—its drowse and shudder, tallow dreams in flicker-light, the shaking of canisters at kitchen table meetings for the paper labor we coughed up our lungs for. We coughed up our lungs. That our tap water now flames, that our land is leased to the horizontal drills white-laddering into the Marcellus Shale. The children now have shoes that shine, though they shed them in summer to wade through the creeks and reach for the slippery fish whose skeletons formed in the Devonian along with ferns and horsetail, seed-bearing plants, trapped gas in shale. They bring to us what they can clutch, sloughing off the rock with the blunt tools of their hands, grasping for fragments where spiny imprints of trilobites still swim. They offer us their fossils as gifts, which crumble into chalk in their small wet hands.

Instructions During Blight

title the poems that will remain
unwritten frequencies
whale song, phylum, mineral
veins stripe stone and ash
shrouding the figures arriving from
harbor the boats sing
elegies to the stripped
bark of northern yew trees
make hollow sounds of homes
press hands into tents into
small silent radios

Study in Light

the long reaching after
our casting shadows
return to who we were
before we buried ourselves
in projection: stand still
shade does not follow
our forms   idiot sundials
reaching for the stain

The Hesitation Waltz

In the levering light, how the objects hum. These rooms divide and then divide. If couch to A, then bookshelves to B. *If one bird flies, the nest is mine.* The paintings hold their own weight, cling to the walls like bone. We have been in the balance for some time, our ears pressed closed to these strands of sound. The waltz begins. A music for mismatched dancers, the halting way we search for our missing hands. We pair up, unroll our once red tongues, now turned the silver blank of mirrors. Here in these endless reflections we finally see ourselves: empty brightness: hard shine of the places we are going: rooms opening into rooms that open into the dance halls of our other desires.

III

Landscape (Interior)

Remainders: what is left in high grasses among the shining bits of glass. Language was no longer mine, words like flames under wet kindling shooting to breathe. Summer spent, concussive. At the goodbye dinner, I wanted "chewed" but it came out "chewn." Not finding same things in same places. And N with his hovering fork—"but these sounds are yours." Glad for the overgrown paths that meet me on the way to the known, the damp moss banks where the old words live. Such solid places to return to—*of*, *and*, and *if*— Paths too into the mind, these ways of not saying, and the finding our way back. Is this the tenement courtyard where we were not to play? This dredged image: sister Gabriella tap-dancing on the gum-cemented sidewalks, bars on the Bronx convent window behind. Let these stringing togethers find what I want back. I will get this back. I conjured the brain as a small thing, wrapped in leaves and the color of agar. It held in the shape of a flame and I cupped my palms to keep it warm and alive, this place I want into, this place I am learning my way around.

*

The light box scours for metal intrusions and porous accretions. Milky white glow of bones from the grey transparence. A cleaning of slates and the longing for time. It was the year of hospitals: paper doll gowns, CAT scan orbitals, cobblestone throat. Hundreds of needling voices, a singular call, pull, this wanting from which a space cannot wrest free. O how the word *enervation* has grown into its meaning. Fear of the asystolic, pen-hover. Here's the thrum, the language at least back, and how it is often and curious in the taxis between: once a building raced by rent vertical with lit stitched boxes—we are always on the cusp of *if only* and *when*—and here I thought, the illumined forms must be sewn with animal gut, rawhide, spiderweave, something not of *us*, in order to close, and to hold.

*

Augury: two birds scan the field for the familiar. Wind and the silver upturn of leaves, bright veins underneath.

Apologia, Early Attempt

I, of course, would like to be blameless (unboxed), blooming always of the possible. My wishes, like yours: to stay alive inside. After your cold shoulder, I turned girl flâneur—neon names of corporations and the aluminum letters— *Claritas*—gleaming from the roof of the Millenium hotel.

*

The mixing of coins into the realm—on our side: a sole navigator of the shallow ledger, our failed names in ink. For your part, refusals of soothing and the jangled joint nervings of mistrust. The item in question hung in the balance, innocent, waiting for *exchange*. Sad circle eating itself as it rounds, and the picture of my hands (anxious ellipticals).

*

Can we come back from this?

*

Regarding the unspoken question between us, please check one or both, depending:

☐ our fault
☐ your fault

*

Talk to me of either (world) and I will endeavor to meet you. Some things are always selfish at their core. Even Charon will ask the dull silver to shine, for him, for the flicker-gleam it will bring for the watertrip.

Weights and Measures

In the city in which I used to love you, love
the sound of scouring clean the metallic
discs of light our reaching toward the stacked
collapse into someone else's days I lived in
shallow breathing rooms, chrysanthemum
walls humming into them someone is always blooming
inward—clang of forks dropped in the singular as speech
or let go loud as stars into the self-conscious city
you go unspent by your rage—dumb
waiter taking up the shaking plates, everything
swinging on its stem, the weighted bodies
of counterbalance I could not cradle
or cup my palms to form a nest to
make any shape of receiving this
flinch and startle required to
hold your language

Note for the Wall at El Tiradito

and when it breaks it breaks at first in bed on the day of ascension and trumpeting
return, sun town parading itself past orange blossoms to the starker buildings of
worship and you have sequestered yourself in darkness to finally hear the sour bells
that mark THE END. After: in your sleep, the wreak of the tape gun firing off its
resolve, a tender wrapping in brown paper of one's fitting shoes, farewell
to the students who have saved your life   a little each day they thought
it was you who gave them   something is missing   when it breaks
thereafter   no landscape that will hold   no table
no one to break the bread   each night   the cardboard boxes contain
all that is partial and left   unbroken   you move about the sleeping giants
not allowed to break   open now   force a closing a smile a way to get
through the new city does not shine   except   here is a house that will have you
here is a book that will keep you   thinking: life will hold something beyond
this for my companion: the sound of splitting   trees from the early storm
shorn   shredded   DOWNED   and the National Guard to arrive
that the boughs here break   that I sleep with my breath so legible
and no one to read the exhalations   what has been held back will no longer
hold   this solid laughter   undig your nails from your palms   even these
mountains crack open   shine me   inside I have been leaning
my shoulder against the stone   machinery   for too long   knelt
at the shrine of the damned   wet ground unconsecrated   this is the day
it breaks   inside   the altar wall stuck through with notes
of the hopeful   one couple comes   troubled by infidelities   thinking
this pilgrimage might break   *open something untried*

Collections

The same scuffed shoes as every Sunday. The listing of light, dust motes dreaming of the shining pews just outside the door. Fear of the metal mesh of confession, the father's mouth pursed and waiting for revelations. *You must think of something.* Think of something.

*

For a nickel the gypsy at Coney Island will tell you your fortune. She is old and leaning slightly forward, waiting for you. Past the Mutoscopes and promise of a girl's long legs. Step up to the tall glass booth for the porcelain cracks in her skin and the feeling that everything is out of your hands. She drops your card into the slot. On the gypsy's floor: the dry husks of bees that found their way in but not out.

*

He has spit on graves, or wanted to. His friend from the old neighborhood has the same story. They're old men now but they still play the game: cutouts sent through parcel post. Mary and the bishops revealing their sins. Cartoons for the fallen, cake stuffed into speechless mouths.

Actual Miles

Break off from this   rootless
architecture measuring the distance:
a slowing on the steps, how the front door breaks
the seal   daily decision of *here here*   is the place to return—
don't return to me this ruined ember, this after
a decade of try how *try* became   such practiced reaching
in the backyard I mocked the mockingbird until
it tired of me   —flew
in the new   city of sirens   smolder and smoke
I will tell them where to put things   a slowing
on the staircase into blind   clearings
this place without birds will be actual—
replica with lesser objects   thoughts are
measured   at first   the house is
pretend   it is not   actual
miles from   the idea of home   a nesting
doll   *where is the light switch?*
in the dark   branches   of the birdless
trees against the windows   are lashes
on the eyes of a sleepy child
god at the window   blinking once   peering in—

Lake Effect

Amber lappings at the banks and the fraying ropes of the useless boats, nets coiled and tucked away until. Softened shards of light wash ashore, beach glass worried over by water's hands. At the dead lake, the fish give the moon their bellies for shine—silver perch, pike, school of bluegill or bream. The algal mats have long been silent: anoxic. This single folded image is no one's salvo. Cast out but not to pull something back.

Amplitude, 3 a.m.

First snowfall and the sound of static. Radio with its mouth taped shut (driveway, idling). The locked door whispers *welcome home* but the quiet holds its coded amplitudes. *You will never again be home.* This is a promise. This is fear made promise through fear. This is your last best your first and almost try at begin, again. Begin again.

Etude for Alternating Hands

No known singing for these days I am half-throated—hand-held
drill, bits whirring into wood. I am learning to level, to shim, to
shore up the walls for winter. At night: the careful etchings onto
storm drains, trees marked with red *X*'s, invisible boys lighting up the
vacant homes already lost to foreclosure. Score of sirens, sandpaper.
Left hand on the strike plate, right hand sounding the shallow
canisters, dead bolts turning over in their brass beds.

Funerary

Bright bonelight, the leanings, and the ones who won't bear you up.
In the aftermath you require too much—your friends for poultice
:: winders of the winding sheet :: this funerary :: this broken silex ::
songs turned dust and mote. Are you unready to lower the ossuary
weight, intern its gleam and cast? In the afterlife what is given is only
what is yours and therefore yours to carry.

List of Last Lines

Into the uncrossed dark

these red shoes stitched under your skin

end stop of the world—Emily

we could call this back

your name swept clean

the wringing of scenery like a sponge

bright bloom of decision

now the strange pageant commences

and the credenza, at least, believes

there are other darknesses

at the coast of industry

calamities arrive in concert

I will say almost anything

do you always follow

instructions for vigil

Study in Light

I've buried these birds
of desire, the knit space
between us held
no promise but this blinding
field of pure decision:
shift of snow, loose sugar slide
from each winter roof
Narcissus tipped its inebriate
bleached and broken blooms
shaking free from roots

The Return

Room here for swarm and sun. The bees burrowing under: hum and stitch to the season. Here is the luxurious real estate of the wild. Rocks holding their prehistoric poses. Lavender becoming itself in the old repetitions, a practiced alchemy into amber.

*

We called the apiaries when the swarms arrived. Five hundred in my chimney surrounding the queen, the house alive with sound. Your apple tree filled with a dark moving stain. We had other lovers then, did not yet know each other by touch. The men arrived at our homes in their medieval masks with equipment for coaxing. The careful collecting and what could not be saved.

*

We wintered. And each turned from house and home.

*

A held-back bow. A well-made quiver. Bright hills a scrim for birds of prey, hawkstains gliding across the knotted grass. One rogue eucalyptus sheds its skin. Tremble dance for the receiver bees. And all we could not see.

*

Opening the chambers. Spill of crackled amber from the combs and the small stitchings into skin. To learn what can come from breakage, to hear again the loud humming.

*

We began with blackberries.

Dream of the Moving Image

Between you and brightness
the ticking of stones under hot sun,
flick-stutterings of silent films, finished
reel flap, tourists gliding, and how
the sculptor's hands shook when he saw
this day: sap bubbling up, cracking open
the wooden skin of his women's arms,
running down, thick and alive, sharp
smell of *inside* flooding the sculpture garden,
and you, student of the visceral
world, shading your eyes from sun to
feel this moment, this coming alive

North Triptych

—after Rothko

To forgo the naming of things. To no longer reach after the horizon. Into the black that shines and all that can not be pushed from the final spaces. What presses in until the wavering becomes a singular altar of your own throat. The martin's inward song.

*

Waveforms of gray and the purpled stain of communions that would not take.

*

Imperfect light but light.

Notes

I

RESIDUE The underground cathedral mentioned in the poem refers to the Catedral de Sal Zipaquirá. The mine has been in use since the third century BC and continues as both a cathedral and a working mine to this day.

ATTEMPTS AT DIVINATION contains a quote from seventeenth-century alchemist Paracelsus.

ESTUARY John R. Stilgoe's *Shallow Water Dictionary: A Grounding in Estuary English* (Princeton Architectural Press, 2004) provided the two quoted passages, and more generally guided the language of this poem. With estuaries and marshes at risk from the effects of global warming, the language of these landscapes risks extinction as well. Stilgoe describes his book as a "salvage operation of words drifting from dictionary language."

JUBILATE: BURDEN, KANSAS owes debts to Christopher Smart's *Jubilate Agno*, Lisa Mahar-Keplinger's beautifully illustrated text *Grain Elevators* (Princeton Architectural Press, 1997), and the U.S. Department of Labor's OSHA report on the explosion of the DeBruce grain elevator. Some language in the poem pulls directly from this report.

WITH A LINE FROM MONTALE takes its last phrase, "which you carry carved in you as your sentence," from Eugenio Montale's poem "The Storm."

II

THE HESITATION WALTZ owes its title to the eponymous painting by René Magritte.

III

Weights and Measures' first line is based on Li-Young Lee's 1991 book title *The City in Which I Love You.*

Note for the Wall at El Tiradito El Tiradito is the only shrine in the United States dedicated to a sinner, a man who purportedly died fighting for the love of a woman. He was buried in unconsecrated ground. The shrine is located in Tucson, Arizona.

Actual Miles owes its title to a Raymond Carver short story.

North Triptych is inspired by the Rothko Chapel in Houston, Texas.

Acknowledgments

Grateful acknowledgement is made to the editors of the following journals, in which some of these poems first appeared:

Colorado Review: "Attempts at Divination," "North Triptych"
Five Fingers Review: "Pietà"
jubilat: "The Orpheus House"
Mid-American Review: "By Water," "St. John's Parish, Bronx,"
    "Walker Evans Meets His Subject (*Grave*, 1936)"
New Letters: "Estuary," "Three Trees"
P-Queue: "Littoral," "7 Girls in Petticoats and Kneesocks (School
    Photo, circa 1920)"
Sentence: A Journal of Prose Poetics: "Jubilate: Burden, Kansas,"
    "Landscape (Interior)"

About the Author

Siobhán Scarry grew up in northern New Jersey. A graduate of the University of Montana's creative writing program, she has published in *Colorado Review, jubilat, New Letters, Sentence: A Journal of Prose Poetics*, and elsewhere. Her prose poems were selected three years running as Editors' Choice in *Mid-American Review's* Fineline Competition for the Prose Poem. She also holds a PhD in literature from SUNY Buffalo, and has published critical essays on 20th-century poetry. She lives and teaches in the Pacific Northwest.

Photograph of Siobhán Scarry by Hélène Cyr.
Used by permission.

Free Verse Editions

Edited by Jon Thompson

13 ways of happily by Emily Carr
Between the Twilight and the Sky by Jennie Neighbors
Blood Orbits by Ger Killeen
The Bodies by Chris Sindt
The Book of Isaac by Aidan Semmens
Canticle of the Night Path by Jennifer Atkinson
Child in the Road by Cindy Savett
Contrapuntal by Christopher Kondrich
Country Album by James Capozzi
The Curiosities by Brittany Perham
Current by Lisa Fishman
Dismantling the Angel by Eric Pankey
Divination Machine by F. Daniel Rzicznek
Erros by Morgan Lucas Schuldt
The Forever Notes by Ethel Rackin
The Flying House by Dawn-Michelle Baude
Instances: Selected Poems by Jeongrye Choi, trans. by Brenda Hillman,
    Wayne de Fremery, and Jeongrye Choi
A Map of Faring by Peter Riley
Pilgrimly by Siobhán Scarry
Physis by Nicolas Pesque, translated by Cole Swensen
Poems from above the Hill & Selected Work by Ashur Etwebi, translated by
    Brenda Hillman and Diallah Haidar
The Prison Poems by Miguel Hernández, translated by Michael Smith
Puppet Wardrobe by Daniel Tiffany
Quarry by Carolyn Guinzio
remanence by Boyer Rickel
Signs Following by Ger Killeen
Summoned by Guillevic, translated by Monique Chefdor
These Beautiful Limits by Thomas Lisk
An Unchanging Blue: Selected Poems 1962–1975 by Rolf Dieter Brinkmann,
    translated by Mark Terrill
Under the Quick by Molly Bendall
Verge by Morgan Lucas Schuldt
The Wash by Adam Clay
We'll See by George Godeau, translated by Kathleen McGookey
What Stillness Illuminated by Yermiyahu Ahron Taub
Winter Journey [Viaggio d'inverno] by Attilio Bertolucci, translated by
    Nicholas Benson

www.ingramcontent.com/pod-product-compliance
Lightning Source LLC
Chambersburg PA
CBHW022040090426
42741CB00007B/1139